HLT
PUBLICATIONS

COMMERCIAL LAW

Suggested Solutions

UNIVERSITY OF LONDON
JUNE EXAMINATION 1990

HLT PUBLICATIONS
200 Greyhound Road, London W14 9RY

Examination Questions © The University of London 1990
Solutions © The HLT Group Ltd 1990

ISBN 1 85352 639 8

British Library Cataloguing-in-Publication.

A CIP Catalogue record for this book is available from the
British Library.

Printed and bound in Great Britain.

FOREWORD

HLT Publications are written specifically with the student in mind. Whether they are studying for A Levels, a degree or professional qualification they will find our publications clear, concise and up-to-date.

All our publications are written by specialists, the majority of whom have direct practical teaching experience. Each year all our materials are carefully reviewed and updated as appropriate.

HLT Publications is the publishing arm of Holborn College, which has experience of over twenty years as an independent college with a current student population of over 2,000. We are ideally placed to understand and respond to the needs of students. Most importantly, we are able to test our publications directly in our own lecture theatres.

Proof of the high quality of our texts is that they are widely used by students at universities, polytechnics and colleges throughout the United Kingdom and overseas, as well as by practitioners seeking an update or overview on recent changes. Given the comprehensive range of topics covered, whatever syllabus you are studying, our texts will be invaluable to you.

Textbooks provide an invaluable foundation and comprehensive introduction to the subject and aim to equip the student with a sound grasp of the basic principles involved. They include discussions of the current state of the law as well as considering practical issues.

Casebooks have been produced as companion volumes to the relevant textbooks, and aim to supplement and enhance students' understanding and interpretation of a particular area of the law, and to provide essential background reading. They contain the appropriate statutes as well as all the important cases, and include extracts from judgments together with detailed commentaries as appropriate.

Revision WorkBooks are a new series of questions and answers for students preparing for law examinations. They are arranged in the order of the topics to which they apply. This valuable revision aid is supported by key points and question analysis for each subject, recent cases and statutes, and concise notes on how to study and plan effective revision strategies.

Suggested Solutions to past examination papers are available for LLB, Bar and Solicitors' Finals examinations. They are available either as single papers covering the last examinations or in packs covering a number of preceding years' examinations. These are not intended as model answers but may be used as both a revision aid and a guide to examination techniques.

Law Update published annually in March/April gives law students at degree and professional levels, and other students with law elements in their courses, a review of the most recent developments in specific subject areas - an essential revision aid for the next examinations. Practitioners seeking a quick update will also find this a useful guide on recent changes.

Publications are available from most academic bookshops or by mail order from the publisher. An order form appears at the back of this book.

HOLBORN COLLEGE COURSES

SPECIALIST DIPLOMAS IN LAW & BUSINESS

Validated by the University of Oxford Delegacy of Local Examinations at degree level.

9 month course.

Diplomas in: Contract Law • Commercial Law • Company Law • Revenue Law • European Community Law • Criminal Law • Evidence • Constitutional Law • English Legal System • Land Law • Organisational Theory • Economics • Accounting and Business Finance • Computer Systems & Information Technology • Maths for Economists • Statistics

Entry: Evidence of sufficient academic or work experience to study at degree level.

FUNDAMENTALS OF BRITISH BUSINESS

Examined internally by Holborn College

To familiarise European and other overseas business studies students with UK business practice. Courses are tailor-made for groups of students on a College to College basis. Courses run for ten to seventeen weeks and permit part-time relevant work experience.

Past courses have included: Aspects of Organisational Behaviour • Marketing • Statistics • Business English & Communication Skills • Economics • International Trade • Company Law

LAW

Examined externally by the University of London.

Three year course.

LLB Law.

Entry: 2 'A' levels grade E and 3 'O' levels.

ACCOUNTING & MANAGEMENT DEGREES

Examined externally by the University of London.

Three year course.

BSc (Econ) Accounting • BSc (Econ) Management Studies • BSc (Econ) Economics & Management Studies

Entry: 2 'A' levels grade E and 3 'O' levels to include Maths and English.

DIPLOMA IN ECONOMICS.

Examined externally by the University of London.

One year full time, two year part time courses.

Completion of the Diploma gives exemption from the first year of the BSc (Econ) Degree programmes reducing them to two years.

Entry: Mathematics and English 'O' level equivalent. Minimum age 18.

THE COMMON PROFESSIONAL EXAMINATION

Examined externally by Wolverhampton Polytechnic.

9 month, 6 month and short revision courses.

Entry: Acceptance by the Professional Body.

THE BAR EXAMINATION

Examined by the Council of Legal Education for non-UK practitioners.

9 month course.

Entry: Acceptance by the Professional Body.

THE SOLICITORS' FINAL

Examined by the Law Society.

6 month re-sit and short revision courses.

Entry: Acceptance by the Professional Body.

THE INSTITUTE OF LEGAL EXECUTIVES FINAL PART 2

Examined by the Institute of Legal Executives.

9 month course and short revision courses.

Entry: Acceptance by the Professional Body.

A & AS LEVEL COURSES

Examined by various UK Boards.

9 month course and short revision courses

Subjects offered: Law • Constitutional Law • Economics • Accounting • Business Studies • Mathematics Pure and Applied • Mathematics and Statistics • Sociology • Government and Politics

Entry: 3 'O' levels.

FULL-TIME, PART-TIME, REVISION & DISTANCE LEARNING

ACKNOWLEDGEMENT

The questions used are taken from past University of London LLB (External) Degree examination papers and our thanks are extended to the University of London for the kind permission which has been given to us to use and publish the questions.

Caveat:

The answers given are not approved or sanctioned by the University of London and are entirely our responsibility.

They are not intended as 'Model Answers', but rather as Suggested Solutions.

The answers have two fundamental purposes, namely:

a) To provide a detailed example of a suggested solution to examination questions, and

b) To assist students with their research into the subject and to further their understanding and appreciation of the subject of Laws.

Note:

Please note that the solutions in this book were written in the year of the examination for each paper. They were appropriate solutions at the time of preparation, but students must note that certain caselaw and statutes may subsequently have changed.

INTRODUCTION

Why choose HLT publications

Holborn College has earned an International reputation over the past ten years for the outstanding quality of its teaching, Textbooks, Casebooks and Suggested Solutions to past examination papers set by the various examining bodies.

Our expertise is reflected in the outstanding results achieved by our students in the examinations conducted by the University of London, the Law Society, the Council of Legal Education and the Associated Examining Board.

The object of Suggested Solutions

The Suggested Solutions have been prepared by College lecturers experienced in teaching to this specific syllabus and are intended to be an example of a full answer to the problems posed by the examiner.

They are not 'model answers', for at this level there almost certainly is not just one answer to a problem, nor are the answers written to strict examination time limits.

The opportunity has been taken, where appropriate, to develop themes, suggest alternatives and set out additional material to an extent not possible by the examinee in the examination room.

We feel that in writing full opinion answers to the questions that we can assist you with your research into the subject and can further your understanding and appreciation of the law.

Notes on examination technique

Although the SUBSTANCE and SLANT of the answer changes according to the subject-matter of the question, the examining body and syllabus concerned, the TECHNIQUE of answering examination questions does *not* change.

You will not pass an examination if you do not know the substance of a course. You *may* pass if you do not know how to go about answering a question although this is doubtful. To do *well* and to guarantee success, however, it is necessary to learn the technique of answering problems properly. The following is a guide to acquiring that technique.

1   *Time*

> All examinations permit only a limited time for papers to be completed. All papers require you to answer a certain number of questions in that time, and the questions, with some exceptions carry equal marks.
>
> It follows from this that you should never spend a disproportionate amount of time on any question. When you have used up the amount of time allowed for any one question STOP and go on to the next question after an abrupt conclusion, if necessary. If you feel that you are running out of time, then complete your answer in *note form*. A useful way of ensuring that you do not over-run is to write down on a piece of scrap paper the time at which you should be starting each part of the paper. This can be done in the few minutes before the examination begins and it will help you to calm any nerves you may have.

2   *Reading the question*

> It will not be often that you will be able to answer every question on an examination paper. Inevitably, there will be some areas in which you feel better prepared than others. You will prefer to answer the questions which deal with those areas, but you will never know how good the questions are *unless you read the whole examination paper.*

You should spend *at least* 10 MINUTES at the beginning of the examination reading the questions. Preferably, you should read them more than once. As you go through each question, make a brief note on the examination paper of any relevant cases and/or statutes that occur to you even if you think you may not answer that question: you may well be grateful for this note towards the end of the examination when you are tired and your memory begins to fail.

3   *Re-reading the answers*

Ideally, you should allow time to re-read your answers. This is rarely a pleasant process, but will ensure that you do not make any silly mistakes such as leaving out a 'not' when the negative is vital.

4   *The structure of the answer*

Almost all examination problems raise more than one legal issue that you are required to deal with. Your answer should:

i)   *identify the issues raised by the question*

        This is of crucial importance and gives shape to the whole answer. It indicates to the examiner that you appreciate what he is asking you about.

        This is at least as important as actually answering the questions of law raised by that issue.

        The issues should be identified in the first paragraph of the answer.

ii)   *deal with those issues one by one as they arise in the course of the problem*

        This, of course, is the substance of the answer and where study and revision pays off.

iii)   *if the answer to an issue turns on a provision of a statute, CITE that provision briefly, but do not quote it from any statute you may be permitted to bring into the examination hall*

        Having cited the provision, show how it is relevant to the question.

iv)   *if there is no statute, or the meaning of the statute has been interpreted by the courts, CITE the relevant cases*

        'Citing cases' does not mean writing down the nature of every case that happens to deal with the general topic with which you are concerned and then detailing all the facts you can think of.

        You should cite *only* the most relevant cases - there may perhaps only be one. No more facts should be stated than are absolutely essential to establish the relevance of the case. If there is a relevant case, but you cannot remember its name, it is sufficient to refer to it as 'one decided case'.

v)   *whenever a statute or case is cited, the title of statute or the name of the case should be underlined*

        This makes the examiner's job much easier because he can see at a glance whether the relevant material has been dealt with, and it will make him more disposed in your favour.

vi)   *having dealt with the relevant issues, summarise your conclusions in such a way that you answer the question*

        A question will often say at the end simply 'Advise A', or B, or C, etc. The advice will usually turn on the individual answers to a number of issues. The point made here is that the final paragraph should pull those individual answers together *and actually give the advice required*. For example, it may begin something like: 'The effect of the answer to the issues raised by this question is that one's advice to A is that ...'

vii)   *related to (vi), make sure at the end that you have answered the question*

For example, if the question says 'Advise A', make sure that is what your answer does. If you are required to advise more than one party, make sure that you have dealt with all the parties that you are required to and no more.

5   *Some general points*

You should always try to get the examiner on your side. One method has already been mentioned - the underlining of case names, etc. There are also other ways as well.

Always write as *neatly* as you can. This is more easily done with ink than with a ball-point.

Avoid the use of violently coloured ink eg turquoise; this makes a paper difficult to read.

Space out your answers sensibly: leave a line between paragraphs. You can always get more paper. At the same time, try not to use so much paper that your answer book looks too formidable to mark. This is a question of personal judgment.

NEVER put in irrelevant material simply to show that you are clever. Irrelevance is not a virtue and time spent on it is time lost for other, relevant, answers.

UNIVERSITY OF LONDON

INTERMEDIATE EXAMINATION

PARTS I & II

for External Students

COMMERCIAL LAW

Thursday, 7 June 1990: 2.30 to 5.30

Answer **FOUR** of the following EIGHT questions.
(Assume that all contracts are governed by English law.)

1   'Modern commercial law is essentially obsessed with two competing policies: on the one hand, affording protection to contracting parties and, on the other, controlling the ways in which parties, in particular sellers and other creditors, can protect themselves.'

To what extent is this statement true?

2   'Agency is an entirely sensible exception to the general doctrine of privity of contract, made necessary by good sense. Commerce could not function well or conveniently without intermediaries. That does not, however, justify the limits to which the agency doctrine is pushed by the further, unwarrantable, doctrine of the undisclosed principal.'

Discuss.

3   'The implied terms in the Sale of Goods Act 1979 are simply a method - though an incomplete and imperfect one - of endeavouring to ensure that the buyer of goods gets what he pays for. They serve a useful function, albeit no doubt they could be improved upon.'

Do the current implied terms work well? Could they be made better?

4   Peelsy plc, a drinks company, places advertisements as follows: 'We sell the widest range of wines, beers and drinks. Details available from our authorised outlets.' Peelsy has representatives at three outlets in Mykindatown: Alphonse and Bruno, who are both managers of shops carrying Peelsy's name; and Capone, the manager of a third shop, which Peelsy bought from Capone and which still trades under the name 'Capone's'. All three managers sign contracts on 1 January 1990 stipulating that they will be employed for a minimum of three years, though Capone's contract also provides that his employment will continue so long as 'Capone's' remains profitable. The contracts forbid the managers from selling products not supplied or ordered by the head office of Peelsy.

Advise Peelsy in the following cases:

a)   Alphonse sells 20 cases of Vin Plonc to Theo, who only agrees to buy it on Alphonse's 'personal guarantee' that it will increase in value by 10 per cent in five months; it does not.

b)   Ulrich runs a grocer's shop near Bruno's shop. He does not normally sell alcoholic drinks. In March, there is a shortage of cocoa, a product which Peelsy does not normally supply. Ulrich tells Bruno that, if he can obtain some cocoa through one of Peelsy's contacts, he will also buy 50 cases of wine and pay Bruno himself £100 for his help. He receives the cocoa and wine, for which he has not paid, and pays Bruno half of the £100 'on account'.

c)   Vivien, Capone's former landlady, normally buys her drinks from another supplier, Squelch; but, in part settlement of Capone's unpaid rent, she orders 100 cans of soft drinks from Capone.

d)   In June, Peelsy decides to sell the three shops to Squelch, who wishes to demolish them and to develop a wine superstore on the best of the three sites, the 'Capone's' site.

5   Slimbo manufactures a run of 100 'superwidgets', which he advertises for orders. He agrees to sell 40 to Bill, in Birmingham, who needs them for his business. Slimbo delivers a crate of 40 to a depot

owned by Harry, an independent road haulier, for 'delivery to be advised'. Harry later tells Slimbo that he has a delivery to make in Birmingham the following day and Slimbo says, 'You may as well drop off that crate at Bill's if you have time.' On the way to Birmingham, Harry's lorry is involved in an accident, after which it is towed back to Harry's depot, with the crate and its contents damaged.

The next day, Slimbo sell 60 superwidgets to Chloe in Cardiff under a contract providing that he is 'to retain title to the goods until paid for'. Chloe makes a down payment for 30 superwidgets. Since Harry's next delivery is in Cardiff, Slimbo tells him to deliver to Chloe the crate which is at his depot; Harry does this.

Slimbo, who has not received any further orders for superwidgets, then becomes insolvent.

Advise the parties.

6   Selim contracts to sell the following goods:

a)   To Barbara, 500 tons Western White Wheat c & f Liverpool; the wheat is shipped from New York on 1 June; on 5 June, the carrying vessel sinks; on 6 June, Selim tenders the shipping documents to Barbara.

b)   To Betty, 1,000 gallons Australian perfume ex ship *Mangel* at Liverpool; Betty fails to pay Selim for a previous cargo (of cork hats, which she has been unable to resell), so Selim orders the master of the *Mangel* to deliver the perfume to Thurstan, a friend of Selim's to whom Selim wishes to make a present of the perfume.

c)   To Billy, 60 chainsaws. Billy contracts to resell them to Tom, and instructs Selim to deliver them to Tom. Six weeks after delivery of the chainsaws, two of Tom's customers complain to Tom that they have been injured because of defects in the chainsaws. Tom recalls all the chainsaws which he has sold, reimburses his customers for their losses and returns the whole consignment to Billy, from whom he claims repayment.

Advise Barbara, Betty and Billy.

7   Delbert, a used car dealer in London, advertises for sale a 1966 Ford Consul, which he describes as being 'in as perfect condition as the day she was made'. Unknown to Delbert, the car was recently in a serious accident while on hire purchase from Finco Ltd to Roger. Roger had sold it to Delbert after repairing it.

Delbert tells Hiram that the car has only had one owner, so Hiram agrees to take it on hire purchase, which Delbert arranges with Finco Ltd.

The agreement between Finco and Hiram states that: 'This contract is made solely between the two parties hereto, no other person having authority to act in any way on behalf of any of the parties. The hirer takes the car as he finds it on inspection, which he agrees to make to satisfy himself of its condition. No liability of any sort is accepted by the creditor for its condition.'

The car regularly breaks down and Hiram incurs a great deal of expenditure having it repaired at Xerxes' garage. Since Finco's office is in Newcastle, Hiram calls in at Delbert's showrooms to inform him that, so far as he is concerned, the deal is off and he wants his money back; the car, he says, is at Xerxes' garage, where Xerxes is keeping it until his bills have been paid.

Advise Hiram.

8   Advise Horatio, who enters into agreement with the Finance-U Co to acquire the following goods, supplied by Denden plc:

a)   A new refrigerator, hire purchase price of £300. Denden has a shortage of official agreement forms, so the basic terms are typed on a piece of paper with a note stating that the transaction is 'on Finance-U Co's usual terms'. A photocopy of the document is handed to Horatio. Two days later, before the refrigerator is delivered, Horatio telephones the manager of Denden's saying that he does not want the refrigerator after all. The manager does nothing, assuming that Finance-U Co will have already signed the agreement, although in fact this is not done until the following day.

b)   A motor mower, hire purchase price £480. The agreement (top copy and an attached carbon copy) is sent by Finance-U Co to Horatio's home to look at. Two days later, Horatio takes it to Denden's premises, where he signs it and leaves both copies. After Horatio has paid £200, Finance-U Co hears that his lawn does not appear to have been cut recently and writes to demand information about the use and whereabouts of the mower. Horatio has been ill and fails to answer the letter or to pay the next two instalments. The mower is kept under a lean-to, where it occasionally gets wet and begins to rust. One night it is damaged by a falling tree in a freak hurricane. The following day, an employee of Finance-U Co calls on Horatio (who is out) and takes the mower away with him.

QUESTION 1

General Comment

A typical essay question based on the competing interests in commercial law; namely the protection to be afforded to the consumer and the degree of protection that should be available to the seller/creditor. Initially this would appear a relatively easy question, but the statement the candidate is asked to comment upon is very widely drawn and the candidate would have to be careful to ensure that close definition of the scope of the essay is applied to prevent too much time being spent on this answer to the detriment of others.

Skeleton Answer

1   Definition of commercial law and scope theory ie:- consumer law, credit transactions, sale of goods, international trade.

2   Origins of the law, ie Common Law, Private Law, Statute Law, Criminal and Civil Law.

3   Origins and development of policy in commercial law. Basic contractual principles.

4   Protection afforded to contracting parties especially consumers.

5   Controls with special reference to protection afforded to sellers and creditors.

6   Comparison of protection for consumers/sellers/creditors.

7   Conclusion - recent developments, excepted contracts.

Suggested Solution

The candidate is required to comment on the truth of the widely drawn quotation 'modern commercial law is essentially obsessed with two competing policies: on the one hand, affording protection to contracting parties and, on the other, controlling the ways in which parties, in particular sellers and other creditors, can protect themselves.

This statement is widely drawn and requires analysis of the origins of commercial law to the present time and the basic contractual principles which underlie all the disparate elements which make up the various relationships between consumers and debtors and their opposite numbers, namely sellers and creditors.

It is well nigh impossible to set out all the categories of contract that make up the generic term 'commercial law' - the law itself is derived from many different sources and is constantly developing to meet the requirements of the increasingly complicated 'consumer society'. Even the term consumer can be ambiguous in this context because, for example, goods (eg a micro-computer) bought for use in a business or in the home may still be 'consumer goods'.

There are common themes that have developed in commercial law over the years but it appears that English Law has developed no comprehensive 'commercial law'; rather developments have been derived in piecemeal fashion from disparate categories of law. For example, common law doctrines, statutory codes, administrative remedies and even some criminal law sanctions.

The proposition herein is that 'modern commercial law' is 'essentially obsessed' with the competing interests of consumers/debtors and those of sellers/creditors. Initially therefore, one must look at some of the categories of individuals and trading entities that the law recognises before one can fully explore the nature of these competing interests. If one accepts the simple proposition that modern commercial law is concerned with two basic forms of contractual arrangement - namely the transfer of ownership title and risks in property for the consideration known as the price or the provision of finance for the purchase of goods and/or services, then one can explore more readily the nature of the competing interests and the development of commercial law. One can then properly assess the competing interests of buyer/debtors and sellers/creditors.

Many common law doctrines and maxims underpin the modern commercial law; but they have been overlain with statute law, precedents and various principles and doctrines from civil and criminal law. Take for example the maxim of caveat emptor (buyer beware); essentially this remains the basis of a commercial contract, the

QUESTION 1 (continued)

responsibility is placed on the buyer to properly investigate and assess the goods offered and to discharge the onus placed upon him in this respect. The consumer has had statutory protection since the Sale of Goods Act 1892 (as amended by the Sale of Goods Act 1979) of certain inalienable rights with regard to consumer contracts; in particular title of the seller, fitness for purpose merchantable quality, corresponding with description etc have been and still remain, the subject of implied terms. The protection afforded by the 'implied terms' of the Sale of Goods Act 1979 has been enhanced by precedents and other supporting statutes derived from civil and criminal law.

Thus, for example, the maxim caveat emptor appears to have been in some respects effectively reversed by s3 of the Misrepresentation Act 1967 and the trader must beware of committing himself to any statement that may amount to a misrepresentation. Section 51(2) Sale of Goods Act 1979 contains a codification of the principles established in the case of *Hadley* v *Baxendale* (1854) Ex 341 to enable the better assessment of the measure of damages under a breach of a contract for the sale of goods: "the measure of damages is the estimated loss directly and naturally resulting in the ordinary course of events from the seller's breach of contract".

Consumer protection is further enhanced by, for example, the statutes controlling the extent to which sellers of goods/services can impose and exercise exclusion clauses over liability for their products and services. Thus the Unfair Contract Terms Act 1977 replaced the controls first contained in the Supply of Goods (Implied Terms) Act 1973. Persons 'dealing as a consumer' (s12(1) UCTA 1977) can claim the protection of the UCTA and the courts will apply the test of 'reasonableness' (s2 and s11 UCTA) to any disputed exclusion clause. The consumer, furthermore, has the benefit of the long succession of precedents developed in the consumer's favour in respect of exclusion clauses under the 'contra preferentum' principles. (Some of the notable examples being *Olley* v *Marlborough Court* [1949] 1 KB 532 and *Thornton* v *Shoe Lane Parking* [1971] 2 QB 163.) Protection does not end at the UCTA; some further recourse may be had to the control by the criminal law of exemption clauses under the Consumer Transactions (Restrictions on Statements) Order 1976 (amended by CT (RS) O 1978) which introduces criminal offences for breaches of s6 UCTA and the Trading Stamps Act 1964.

It is obvious that no coherent code has been developed and that as previously stated the law has developed in a piecemeal fashion. Sales and purchases of goods are not the only form of the modern commercial law; the provision of finance by hire purchase and the various methods of credit are another important aspect that fall to be considered under the main proposition. There are obviously policies that have developed in relation to modern commercial law and their obvious aim is to control the relationships between sellers/buyers and debtors/creditors. To what extent it is true to say that commercial law is 'obsessed' with these competing policies is difficult to ascertain. It may be fairer to state that the commercial law is developing 'pendulum' fashion in response to the changing needs and requirements of the opposing parties in commercial transactions, rather than as a result of deliberate and effective policy making. That, for example, consumer interests will be perceived as being in need of protection in some respect; that protection may be afforded as the result of new legislation; too much bias in favour of the consumer will result and the pendulum will then 'swing' in favour of the creditor/seller (for example through precedent, amending legislation or failure to effect new legislation favourable to the consumer, but prejudicial to sellers) to redress the bias and restore the equilibrium.

As a result of the way in which commercial law has developed, the lack of direction and discernible policy has presented many difficulties. An examination of the law relating to credit and the provision of credit seems to indicate that present policy is directed at establishing a firm position where both parties to a transaction are adequately (but not overly) protected and can lawfully and commercially pursue their bargain. This development appears to be mirrored by recent developments in the law relating to the sale of goods, consumer protection and product liability.

Both parties to a commercial transaction require some protection and remedies to redress any injustices against them; this applies to credit and sale of goods contracts alike. Both parties have obligations and rights; the key policy objective should be equality of treatment and not an 'obsessive' interest in propagating the conflicts that arise. Credit transactions and the provision of credit should afford both creditor and debtor ample commercial scope to make agreements and to terminate such agreements. The 1971 Crowther Committee (Cmnd 4596) expressed concern about 'the serious anomalies arising from the division of credit transactions into legally distinct compartments and from failure to accord a uniform treatment to a range of security devices all designed to achieve the same objective'. The recommendations of the Crowther Committee favoured a policy of 'uniformity' and rationalisation of the law of security; in order to license and regulate credit provision and protect both debtor and creditor's interest.

QUESTION 1 (continued)

The result of the Report of the Crowther Committee was the White Paper 'Reform of the Law on Consumer Credit' and the much acclaimed piece of legal draftsmanship The Consumer Credit Act 1974 (CCA 1974). The key concept in the CCA is that of 'Regulated Agreements' (ie Consumer credit agreements or consumer hire agreements, other than exempt agreements - s189 CCA). The Act came into force gradually and was finally fully in force by 19th May 1985. The Act has proven itself to be forward looking and versatile and still regulates credit agreements even those of more recent origin (cash-point dispenser cards for example).

In conclusion, whilst the modern consumer law does contain, by its very nature competing interests, the policy regulating its present form seeks to balance out the respective interests and to maintain the equilibrium that has long been striven for. The law has developed in a rather 'hotch-potch' fashion, but at present it is not true to regard the equilibrium created by statutes, precedents, private, civil and criminal law as 'obsessive' or 'divisive'. Both parties to a commercial transaction have adequate safeguards and remedies to enable equitable and profitable commerce.

QUESTION 2

General Comment

A difficult question that concentrates on a specific aspect of the law of agency and relates it to general contractual principles. The unprepared candidates would find this difficult in the extreme; particularly if he was unfamiliar with the basic law relating to privity of contract.

Skeleton Answer

1   Origins of principle of agency and undisclosed principal.

2   Development of doctrine.

3   Privity of contract generally.

4   Statement of doctrine.

5   Is the doctrine 'unwarrantable'?

6   Why must the doctrine prevail?

Suggested Solution

In the modern commercial law it is not always possible or expedient for the parties to a contract to meet personally or to contract in their personal or corporate capacity directly with one another. Agency in all its various and extended forms allows the proper functioning of contracts of this nature and if operated successfully can benefit all three parties; namely the principal, the agent and the person with whom the contract is made by the principal. It is possible, therefore, to see the logic in the proposition that 'agency is an entirely sensible exception' to the general doctrine of privity of contract, made necessary by 'good sense' and that 'commerce could not function without it' (ie Agency).

Some statement of the general principles of agency are relevant when exploring the proposition that the fact that agency is an exception to the general rules relating to privity of contract and that the doctrine of 'undisclosed' principal is 'unwarrantable' as an extension of the former fact. The general rule in agency is that a disclosed principal is not bound by any act of his agent which is outside the scope of the agent's implied or apparent authority *Sorrell* v *Finch* [1977] AC 728. This holds true unless the principal in fact authorised the agent to do the act or ratified it.

The doctrine of the undisclosed principal can be broadly stated thus; an undisclosed principal may sue or be sued on any contract made on his behalf, or in respect of money paid or received on his behalf, by his agent acting within the scope of his actual authority. *Thomson* v *Davenport* (1829) 9 B & C. However, the rights of the undisclosed principal to sue, and his liability to be sued on a contract made by his agent may be excluded if inconsistent with the terms of the contract, express or implied. There was an attempt earlier this century to establish precedent for the fact that a contract is that of the undisclosed principal, just as in cases where the principal is disclosed, eg *Keighley Maxsted & Co* v *Durant* [1901] AC 240. The reliability of such cases is now in some doubt and according to Barsted on Agency (p313) the doctrine of the undisclosed principal 'even as an exception to the general rules of the privity of contract is "unusual" ' since the tertius is not mentioned nor indeed contemplated by one of the parties, and furthermore takes liabilities as well as rights.

The doctrine of the undisclosed principal is best explained in the terms as being an essential commercial convenience but that the justice of the principal receiving (in some cases) a benefit without incurring a liability is disputable. It is important to distinguish situations where the principal is disclosed but not named from those where there is total non-disclosure of the existence of a principal; in the latter cases the third party would no doubt consider themselves to be contracting with the agent and have no knowledge of the principal. The understatement of the doctrine of the undisclosed principal is that the principal intervenes on the contract of the agent. See for example *Spurr* v *Cass* 5 LRQB 656 where S, a solicitor, practised in the name of S & G; C was also a solicitor, but acted as clerk to S. Held, that S, being the real principal, was entitled to sue alone upon a contract made in the name of the firm.

QUESTION 2 (continued)

An example of a contract where the undisclosed principal intervened on the agent's contract and was subsequently sued can be taken from *Kinahan & Co Ltd* v *Parry* [1910] 2 KB 389 where A appointed B as manager of an hotel owned by A and the licence was taken out in the name of B. A told B to order spirits from a certain brewery only, but B disregarded this instruction and ordered whisky from C. Held: A was liable to C for the price of the whisky. Perhaps the most celebrated case in this respect being *Watteau* v *Fenwick* [1893] 1 QB 346 where it was held that the principal was liable to pay for cigars ordered by the licensee and manager of an hotel who carried on the business in his own name. The court held it was within the authority usually confided to the manager of an hotel to purchase cigars on credit, despite the fact the manager had been expressly forbidden so to do by the principal.

Grievances in law about the question of the undisclosed principal usually arise when the undisclosed principal succeeds in getting a third party to do something because he employs an agent and remains undisclosed himself. Thus, as for example, where a person bought some land which he knew the owner would not sell to him but was entitled to enforce the contract on the grounds that the contract was assignable, *Dyster* v *Randall and Sons* [1926] Ch 932 (a decision that has been much criticised subsequently).

The grounds why the doctrine of the undisclosed principal may be regarded as unwarrantable were adequately stated in *Watteau* v *Fenwick* by Wills J (at pp348-349). 'Once it is established that the defendant was the real principal the ordinary doctrine as to agent and principal applies - that the principal is liable for all the acts of the agent which are not within the authority usually confided to an agent of that character ... Otherwise in every case of undisclosed principal ... the secret limitation of authority would prevail and defeat the action of the person dealing with the agent and then discovering that he was an agent and had a principal.

To conclude the doctrine of undisclosed principal is a necessary if dubious extension of the doctrine of privity of contract because otherwise there would be no way of limiting the extent of the latter doctrine. So many factors (for example the degree of knowledge of the third party, the legal/illegal intention of the agent, the capacity of the agent etc) could otherwise prevail and create even greater problems - the undisclosed principal in this respect represents the 'lesser of two evils'.

QUESTION 3

General Comment

A relatively straightforward essay for the well prepared candidate. The obvious problem is to consider how much the examiner requires the candidate to demonstrate a knowledge of the intricacies of the Sale of Goods Act 1979 implied terms and how much time is to be devoted to discussion of the effectiveness of the terms in practice.

From the phrasing of the question it appears that a broad brush approach is required in relation to the detail of the implied terms themselves; and that the examiner wishes the candidate to concentrate on the business efficacy of the terms and recent attempts to overhaul them (bearing in mind they have been in operation, virtually unchanged since the original 1893 Sale of Goods Act).

Some detailed examination, therefore, of the advantages and disadvantages of the implied terms should be followed by some effective recommendations for the improvement thereon.

Skeleton Answer

1   Terms, Conditions and Warranties - 'Inalienable Rights'.

2   Origins of the present implied terms - Caveat Emptor.

3   The 1979 Sale of Goods Act, Implied Terms in context.

4   Particular advantages of present implied terms.

5   Particular disadvantages of present implied terms.

6   Recent developments and proposals for the future.

7   Suggestions for improvement - conclusion.

Suggested Solution

Generally speaking, the courts will not enquire as to the business efficacy of a contract made between two individuals or trading entities unless certain conditions prevail, for example, the intention of the parties is unclear or there was some misrepresentation. It is generally accepted there are three major categories of contractual terms; namely conditions, warranties and inominate terms (sometimes referred to as intermediate stipulations).

To describe these briefly in the same order as above, conditions are vital or major terms which go to the 'root of the contract', breach of which entitles the innocent party to treat the contract as ended and to claim damages. Warranties are subsidiary or minor terms, breach of which entitles the innocent party to damages only. Section 61 of the Sale of Goods Act 1979 defines a warranty as being 'collateral to the main purpose' of the contract.

The third category referred to above - 'inominate' or intermediate terms, originated in their present form from the decision in the *Hong Kong Fir Case* (1961) and were affirmed as such in *Bunge* v *Tradax* (1981) by Lord Scarman. An inominate term is one, the effect of non-performance of which the parties expressly (or as is more usual) impliedly agree will depend on the nature and consequences of the breach. Prior to these decisions it was widely thought that terms in a contract could only be conditions or warranties. In *Cehave* v *Bremer* (1975) the doctrine of inominate terms was extended to contracts for the sale of goods where an express term that goods were to be 'shipped in good condition' were in effect an intermediate stipulation.

In contracts for the sale of goods we are primarily concerned with the former categories, namely conditions and warranties; the reason for this being that firstly, where breach of condition is proved the consumer can repudiate the contract (subject to s11(4) in sale of goods cases) even though no actionable misrepresentation is proven or alleged. Secondly, the honest belief of the trader is no defence to an action for damages for breach of condition or warranty unlike the provisions of s2(1) Misrepresentation Act 1967.

QUESTION 3 (continued)

The Sale of Goods Act 1893 ss12-15 introduced certain implied terms which benefited the consumer and strengthened rights and remedies against the seller. The Supply of Goods (Implied Terms) Act 1973 amended these in favour of the consumer and The Sale of Goods Act 1979 incorporated the implied terms as ss12-15 also. The statutory rights embodied in these ss12-15 SOGA 1979 are generally regarded as 'inalienable' and (in particular the provisions of s12) cannot be contracted out of by the consumer. Some statutory and common law restrictions on contracting out of ss13-15 are dealt with under s6 of the Unfair Contract Terms Act 1977.

The proposition herein is that the implied terms of the Sale of Goods Act 1979 are an 'incomplete and imperfect' method of 'endeavouring to ensure that the buyer of goods gets what he pays for'. In essence this sums up the rationale behind both the 1893 and 1979 Sale of Goods statutes, but it represents an over-simplification of the complex legal draftsmanship and motivation behind these sections. The proposition continues that 'no doubt they could be improved upon'; this belies the longevity (albeit with some slight amendment) of the sections since their introduction in 1893 and the fact that they are substantially the same now as then.

The Sale of Goods Act 1979 does not actually contain a definition of 'condition' but s11(3) explains the term by reference to its legal effect. Conditions are therefore given their usual meaning (ie terms that go to the 'root' of the contract) and are distinguished from warranties by the remedies available for breach; in the case of breach of condition repudiation, rejection of any goods supplied and damages for breach, in the case of a warranty being breached damages for quantifiable loss being the remedy.

Some reference, without undue attention to detail, is necessary to the actual provisions of ss12-15 SOGA 1979 in order to consider the proposition that they merely ensure the consumer gets what he pays for and to consider if improvement is possible.

Section 12 SOGA 1979 contains an implied condition on the part of the seller that, in the case of a sale, he has a right to sell the goods, and in the case of an agreement to sell he will have such a right at the time the property is to pass. The section also contains implied warranties of freedom from undisclosed encumbrances and the right (s12(2)) to quiet possession of the goods. This applies to all contracts. Section 13 SOGA 1979 contains an implied condition in a contract for the sale of goods by description, there is an implied condition that the goods will correspond with the description; and in a contract for the sale of goods by sample as well as description, a condition that the goods must correspond with both (s13(1). Section 13 applies to all contracts as does s12 and not just to sales made by traders to consumers.

Section 14 SOGA 1979 applies to sales 'made in the course of a business' by the seller and contains an implied condition that 'goods supplied under such a contract are of merchantable quality' (with the exception of defects specifically drawn to the buyer's attention and defects which examination by the buyer before purchase ought to reveal)'. Additionally, 'where the seller sells goods in the course of a business and the buyer expressly or by implication makes known to the seller any particular purpose for which the goods are being bought, there is an implied condition that goods supplied under the contract are reasonably fit for the purpose ... except ... where the buyer does not rely on the skill or judgement of the seller.' (s14(3) SOGA 1979).

Finally s15, SOGA 1979 covers sales by sample where there are implied conditions that the bulk shall correspond with the sample in quality and that the buyer shall have reasonable opportunity of checking this; and that the goods shall be free from any defect rendering them unmerchantable which would not be apparent on reasonable examination of the sample.

Taking all these implied terms together it is apparent that a comprehensive protection is afforded to the consumer and that with other related legislation, in particular the UCTA 1977, these rights cannot be overridden or contracted out of. It cannot therefore be realistic to describe the terms as 'incomplete and imperfect'. The parties are free to make the bargain they choose in the way they choose, doctrines such as 'caveat emptor' still apply; as, for example, where examination takes place and defects should be discovered (s14) but the consumer is protected from unscrupulous dealing by the seller and from the ambiguities that inevitably arise in commercial consumer sales.

These sections are inter-related and form a cumulative protection of the consumer's interests. The best example of this being the inter-relationship between ss13 and 14 by examining the case of *Arcos* v *Ronaasen* [1933] AC 470. Section 14 implies conditions as to the quality and fitness for purpose of goods for a particular purpose. It is of course possible for goods to be of 'merchantable quality' and fit for their purpose within s14 and yet not

QUESTION 3 (continued)

to correspond with their description under s13. In *Arcos* v *Ronaasen* the buyer ordered a quantity of stoves 1/2 inch thick to make cement barrels, the seller knew this purpose. A fractional deviation in size from the buyer's specification was held by the House of Lords to entitle the buyer to reject for breach of s13 even though the goods were merchantable within the contractual specification. The mere fact that the buyer has suffered no damage does not prevent him from rejecting the goods.

The implied terms have not remained static since the 1893 statute; in particular two important modifications have improved them to the advantage of the consumer. The 1973 Supply of Goods (Implied Terms) Act reworded and rearranged the original 1893 s14 and these amendments were incorporated into the 1979 SOGA s14. Section 14(1) begins with the statement of the general principle of caveat emptor, then follows the worded implied condition that goods are of merchantable quality s14(2), and finally the reworded condition that goods are fit for their purpose, s14(3).

In particular, s14(3) represents an improved and simplified provision when compared with the old s14(2) because it is no longer limited to sales by description but covers all 'sales in the course of a business' (the latter being defined to include a 'profession the activities of any government department... or local or public authority') and s14(3) applies even if the seller has not previously dealt in goods of a similar kind or does not normally deal in such goods.

The present interpretation of s14(3) was established in *Henry Kendall & Sons* v *Wm Lillico & Sons Ltd* where the House of Lords stressed that where goods are bought for their normal and obvious purpose, then in the absence of anything to the contrary, the implied condition applies although the buyer has done nothing to indicate the purpose for which they are required. Additionally, the old proviso that there was no condition of fitness for purpose if goods were sold under a patent or trade mark has been deleted from the SOGA 1979. It had already lost most of its meaning (*Baldry* v *Marshall* [1925] 1 KB 260).

Secondly, only three years ago (1987) the Law Commission published a report on the sale and supply of goods (Law Comm No 160, Cmnd 137) which proposed certain developments and proposals; chief amongst these being to replace the statutory definition of 'merchantable quality' by one of 'acceptable quality'. The definition of acceptable quality was to consist of two elements; a basic principle that goods sold or supplied under a contract should be such as would be 'acceptable' to a reasonable person and that there should be a list of aspects of 'quality' any of which could be important in a particular case (eg appearance, finish, fitness of goods for all their common purposes, safety, durability and freedom from minor defects). The Law Commission also proposed that a consumer should not lose the right to reject goods merely because he has signed an 'acceptance note'.

The draft Bill that has resulted from these reports and developments may introduce some more balance between the 'fitness for purposes' and what Atiyah describes as 'non functional aspects of merchantability' - but the same author is of the opinion that 'in general it does not seem likely that the changes proposed by the draft Bill will make much difference to the law ... the concept of 'acceptable quality' ... has even less genuine meaning than the concept of 'merchantable quality' and must be fleshed out by the case law in the various circumstances." (p168 Sale of Goods - P.S. Atiyah).

In conclusion then, despite their great age, and the fact that they have remained relatively unchanged, the implied conditions of the SOGA 1979 do not appear to be either 'incomplete or imperfect'. Of course their function of ensuring the buyer gets what he pays for is a useful one; the conditions ensure this in a comprehensive fashion by the way they inter-relate with one another and with other supporting statutes. The Law Commission and learned writers appear to concur that they work well in practice and are hard-pushed to improve them.

QUESTION 4

General Comment

A question devoted to the subject of agency in its various forms. Relatively straightforward providing the candidate observes the question format and concentrates the appropriate part of the answer in the correct section. A tendency to cover too much detail in any one section could prove detrimental to the timing of the other sections.

Skeleton Answer

1   Definition Agency generally.

2   How agency arises - duties, obligations of the agent.

3   Holding out as agent. Agency by estoppel. Duty of agent not to make secret profit, duty to account.

Suggested Solution

Many commercial transactions in the field of commerce are conducted through agents who act as intermediaries and represent the interests of their principals in the conduct of the principal's business. The essential point to be borne in mind is that the relationship between agent and principal is essentially a binding contractual one which imposes upon both parties rights, duties and obligations. In this example, we are told that the trading relationship established between the drinks company (Peelsy Plc) and it's agents Alphonse (A) Bruno (B) and Capone (C) is a fixed term contract for three years; although Capone has an additional element in that his agency is stated in the contract to "continue so long as Capone's remains profitable". The contracts given to A, B and C forbid them to sell products not 'supplied' or 'ordered' by their Peelsy head office. In all four parts of the question we are asked to advise the parent company (P).

a)   A has agreed to sell 20 cases of Vin Plonc to T and has given a personal assurance that the wine will increase in value by 10 per cent over five months. This guarantee, it must be stressed, is a personal one; at no time does Peelsy appear to have incorporated this into their agency contract with A or other agents.

A is under a contractually binding agreement to sell Peelsy's products, presumably in return he is given his commission on sales, marketing support and the various other incentives available to commercial agents. What needs to be considered is the nature and extent of A's agency with Peelsy.

A has an express contract and can sell products supplied by or ordered from Peelsy. Assuming Vin Plonc falls into one or both of these categories, then A is authorised to sell the product. The general nature of a contractual agency is that the principal (P) invests the agent (A) with actual authority to act on behalf of P. When A has carried out his duties to the best of his abilities then he is entitled to his remuneration under the contract of agency, but must then leave the third party with whom he has contracted on his principal's behalf to assume that the contract was between P and the third party. The agent has actual 'express' authority to perform acts specifically referred to in the agency contract, and he (A) has 'usual' authority to bind his principal to any act done, or contract made by A if it is necessary for or reasonably incidental to carrying out the authority expressly given to A, or is of a type that someone in A's trade or profession usually does have authority to make (*Watteau* v *Fenwick* [1893] 1 QB 346).

However, the agent is not entitled to exceed these 'express' and 'usual' authorities and bind the principal to contracts that the principal has not authorised or has no knowledge of. So whilst it may be usual or express that A does his best to promote 'Vin Plonc' to customers, the giving of a 'personal guarantee' that it will increase in value in a short time period is outside his express contractual agency and also exceeds his presumed or usual authority. The agent's implied duties (over and above his express contractual duties to his principal) are to act in good faith in pursuance of the principal's interest, a duty to account, to make full disclosure of all material facts and not to exceed his authority or make a secret profit (any such profit to be accounted for).

In the giving of a personal guarantee without making full disclosure to his principal, A has exceeded his authority. He does not appear to be acting in the interests of P and in the event that T decides to

QUESTION 4 (continued)

sue on the 'personal guarantee' P would be an undisclosed principal. Accordingly, P has the option to either ratify the guarantee (in which case he (A) would have had to have expressly named P at the time the contract with T was made (*Keighley, Maxsted & Co* v *Durant* [1901] AC 240)) and P will have to unequivocally adopt all of A's actions after full disclosure thereof by A.

It seems unlikely that P will wish to ratify A's actions as they are to his detriment and A did not name P when the contract was made; accordingly, if T decides to sue, P and T are entitled to hold A personally liable on his personal guarantee (see *Mercantile Credit Co* v *Hamblin* [1965] 2 QB 242).

b)   Clearly B, as agent of Peelsy is only expressly authorised under the contract he has signed, to sell goods 'ordered' or 'supplied' from Peelsy. Ulrich has requested B to obtain cocoa through one of P's contacts; so we do not know if the goods (ie the cocoa) are ordered directly from or supplied by P.

The agency of B would normally be limited to his express (ie 'actual' contractual) or implied (ie 'usual') authority. Peelsy appears to be a general vendor of drinks of all varieties and makes and has placed advertisements to this 'effect we sell the widest range of wines, beers and drinks, details available from our authorised outlets'. B is an authorised outlet for these purposes. We are told however, that despite the wide range of drinks sold by Peelsy through its authorised outlets, that the cocoa requested by U in March is not normally supplied by them.

Thus we can assume that B has exceeded his actual and usual authority on two counts; possibly even three and is therefore in breach of his agency contract with P. He has agreed to approach 'P's contacts' and obtain cocoa, usually outside P's trading sphere and he has received a secret profit (albeit only 1/2 the agreed amount) from U. Additionally, B appears to allow U to take wine without paying for it and this is a possible fourth breach of agency.

Taking all these facts together it is obvious that B is not acting in the interests of P, that he does not hesitate to breach his actual and usual agency authority, that he has not made full disclosure of his actions (by approaching P's contacts and obtaining cocoa to supply U) and that, most importantly, he has made a secret profit and has not observed his implied duty to account therefore to P.

These flagrant and repeated breaches of contract are fatal to B's agency contract with Peelsy. B is in breach of several contractual and implied duties of agency; not least amongst these the refusal to obey the lawful instructions of the principal and is therefore liable in damages to his principal (*Cohen* v *Kittell* (1889) 22 QBD 680). Additionally, he has permitted a conflict of interest to develop between his personal interest and the duty of full disclosure to the principal. In this case the principal may set aside the transaction for wine and cocoa with U and claim any profit (£50) made by B. In *Boardman* v *Phipps* [1967] 2 AC 46, the Court of Appeal held that an agent who makes a secret profit is in breach of the duty of good faith to the principal and such secret profit must be accounted for and is recoverable at law by the principal (*Lucifero* v *Castel* (1887) 3 TLR 371).

Lastly, B appears to have breached the duty not to misuse confidential information acquired as a result of agency (*Robb* v *Green* [1895] 2 QB 315) in using 'contacts' properly belonging to P. P can sue for breach of agency, require the handing over of the secret profit, seek damages against B for breach and possibly require B to pay personally for the wine and cocoa not paid for by U.

c)   Capone has sold V some soft drinks which were presumably supplied to him by Peelsy head office. The problem C faces is whether he is using his agency contract to satisfy a personal debt; this appears to be the case. C has not made full disclosure and the 'set-off' he has allowed against his debt to his former landlady on the drinks could amount once again to the making of a secret profit.

This may not prove fatal to C's agency contract and he may be able to claim his remuneration (ie - commission) from Peelsy if he can repay the debt to Peelsy and can prove he has substantially performed his contract (*Rimmer* v *Knowles* (1874) 30 LT 496).

However, a major duty of an agent is to keep proper accounts of all transactions entered into on his principal's behalf and to keep 'agency money' separate from his own. Roskill RJ said in *Aluminium Industrie Vaassen BV* v *Romalpa Aluminium*

QUESTION 4 (continued)

'If an agent lawfully sells his principal's goods, he stands in a fiduciary relationship to his principal and remains accountable to his principal for those goods and their proceeds.'

If he does not keep 'agency money' and his own separate, there is a presumption the whole amount belongs to the principal. In any event it appears that C will have to account to Peelsy and at least repay the balance of the soft drinks sold to V.

d)   This situation requires us to look at the agency - principal relationship from the principal's point of view. The mutual responsibilities of the agency contract are to a greater extent reciprocal; just as the principal can expect the agent to make full disclosure; so the agent can expect a reciprocal duty from the principal.

We have already been informed that Squelch is the rival of Capone's and by implication Squelch must be in competition with the three outlets who act as agents for Peelsy. The sell off by Peelsy to Squelch who intend to demolish all shops and construct a wine superstore on Capone's site amounts to a breach of the agency contract by Peelsy, the principal in this case.

Furthermore, the promises embodied in Capone's contract (originally bought out by Peelsy) that he can continue to trade under his own name and that the contract will continue so long as 'Capone's remains profitable', have also been broken as well as the original three year trading agreement in A, B and C's cases.

All things being equal, and treating P's breach as if none of the problems referred to above had occurred, then A, B and C are entitled to damages for breach of their contract. They are also entitled to an indemnity against P for any expenses and losses incurred as a result of their acting on their principal's behalf - so for example, purchase of leases, advertising, stock in trade etc, can all be claimed by A, B and C (see eg *Hichens, Harrison, Woolston & Co* v *Jackson & Sons* [1943] AC 266.

Additionally, the agents are entitled to claim remuneration from the principal as by contract this has been expressly agreed; so their damages will consist of loss of remuneration and profits if the sell off goes ahead and the wine superstore is built (*John Meacock & Co* v *Abrahams* [1956] 3 All ER.) This is a fixed term contract in the case of A and B; in C's case he may be able to claim what is known as 'continuing commission' as he had an agreement that his employment would continue 'so long as he continued to trade profitably'. As he appears to be so doing even the termination of the agency contract cannot prevent him claiming, as this kind of commission depends on the construction of the contract. (See *Wilson* v *Harper, Son & Co* [1908] 2 Ch 370 where the agent's executors were entitled to receive commission after the death of the agent because the contract stated commission was payable 'as long as we do business'.

Finally, all three agents who are entitled to claim an indemnity or remuneration or both can exercise a lien against goods of the principal which are in their lawful possession as agents until their claims as agents are met; the lien will probably be a 'general' lien arising from the trade usage so it will be exercisable over stock in trade, equipment, etc.

QUESTION 5

General Comment

A question that concentrates on the real remedies available to a bona fide purchaser against an insolvent seller. We are asked to advise all parties, so apart from buyers and seller we need to consider the role played by the independent carrier (Harry). Basic contractual principles govern the making of the contracts. The second contract contains an important 'retention of title' clause.

Skeleton Answer

1   Making a contract, duties of buyer and seller, ownership and risk.

2   Delivery to independent carrier, status of carrier in relation to contract, specific goods.

3   Separate contracts, different buyers, 'delivery to be advised', property, risk and title.

4   Second contract to Chloe, quantity incorrect, conditional contract retention of title clause, damaged goods.

5   Remedies of buyer against insolvent seller for non-delivery and damaged goods.

Suggested Solution

Slimbo appears to have entered into a contractual arrangement with Bill and Chloe to sell them widgets; we are expressly told that Bill requires the widgets for his business but no mention is made in either case that time is to be of the essence in the delivery thereof. The contract with Bill appears to have resulted from the adverts placed by Slimbo. We are given no information as to how the contract with Chloe is arrived at. The contracts appear to both be 'one off' contracts and do not seem to form part of any instalment contract for sale and delivery. The goods which are the subject of the contract with Bill appear to be 'specific goods' as defined by s61(1) Sale of Goods Act 1979 ie 'goods identified and agreed upon at the time a contract of sale is made'. In Bill's case the goods have been manufactured and advertised for sale; 40 of the 100 manufactured have been set aside from the remainder and delivered to an independent carrier for onward delivery to Bill. Thus they are identified and agreed upon by both parties at the time of the contract.

However, the 60 widgets sold the subsequent day to Chloe are sold under a condition, namely that Slimbo is to retain title to the goods until paid for. Chloe, we are told, has made a down payment for 30 widgets. It may well be that half of Chloe's 60 required widgets are specific goods (as defined above) but it seems more likely that all 60 are merely 'unascertained goods' in that they are not identified and agreed upon at the time of the contract, and they require some act of subsequent appropriation for their identification. By s16 SOGA 1979 property in unascertained goods cannot pass until they become ascertained eg *Re Wait* [1927] 1 Ch 606.

Having determined the nature of the goods under the respective contracts, it is necessary to examine when, if at all, the property as referred to in the SOGA 1979 (ie the ownership of the goods) passes to the purchasers and when the risk attached to the goods is passed from seller to buyer. The SOGA uses the word title synonymously with 'ownership' and it uses the phrases 'transfer of property' and 'property passes' to denote transfer of ownership. Section 20 SOGA provides that risk (of loss of goods from trader to consumer) passes with property, ie risk of loss or damage to goods passed to the consumer when ownership passes to him with three exceptions:

1)   the parties may expressly or impliedly agree otherwise;

2)   where delivery has been delayed through the fault of one party (the party at fault takes the risk of any loss that might not otherwise have occurred);

3)   the party in possession, being a bailee of goods, is liable at common law if he is negligent.

In the case of the 40 widgets sold to Bill, the goods are ascertained; the basic fundamental rule concerning the transfer of property is that property 'in goods passes when the parties intend it to pass' SOGA s17.

QUESTION 5 (continued)

However, the contract here appears to be silent as to the parties intention and the circumstances surrounding the contract appear indecisive and complicated by the fact that delivery has been made by Slimbo to Harry (an independent carrier) and on condition 'that delivery is to be advised'. Delivery to an independent carrier is covered by SOGA s32(1).

> 'where in pursuance of a contract of sale the seller is authorised or required to send the goods to the buyer, delivery of goods to a carrier (whether named by the buyer or not), for the purpose of transmission to the buyer is prima facie to be a delivery of the goods to a buyer'.

However, s32(2) covers the situation where the seller makes a contract with an independent carrier on behalf of the buyer "the seller must make such contract with the carrier on behalf of the buyer as may be reasonable, having regard to the nature of the goods and to other circumstances of the case. If the seller omits to do so, and the goods are lost or damaged in the course of transit, the buyer may decline to treat the delivery to the carrier as a delivery to himself, or may hold the seller responsible in damages". See *Thomas Young & Sons* v *Hobson & Partners* (1949) 65 TLR 365.

What constitutes 'delivery' is defined by s61 SOGA 'voluntary transfer of possession from one person to another', so where the seller is authorised to send the goods via independent carrier, delivery to the carrier is prima facie. delivery to the consumer s32(1) SOGA. Delivery to a carrier does not affect the buyer's rights to examine and reject the goods. Generally speaking, time is not of the essence in contracts for the sale of goods unless a contrary intention can be derived from the terms of contract (see s10 SOGA). It may be that Bill who is stated to 'need' the widgets for his business has stipulated delivery time to be of the essence. Usually the place of delivery is the consumer's place of business (SOGA s29(2)), the consumer does not have to accept part only of the goods.

Bill is awaiting delivery of the widgets 'to be advised' but as Harry's lorry is damaged he never receives them or is advised of their 'delivery'. So that, even though delivery to a carrier by the seller usually amounts to 'delivery', in this case Slimbo has failed to deliver. Additionally, Bill has not had the opportunity to examine the goods as allowed for in s34 SOGA. It would appear therefore that, despite the fact that delivery to a carrier normally amounts to constructive delivery, in this case because delivery is 'to be advised' and it has not been, the property in the goods has not passed from Slimbo to Bill. Section 27 SOGA provides that

> 'it is the duty of the seller to delivery the goods and of the buyer to accept and pay for them, in accordance with the terms of the contract of sale'.

Slimbo is in breach of this obligation to deliver and his subsequent actions disposing of the goods to Chloe, despite their being damaged, compound the breach - accordingly Bill can pursue a claim for damages for breach of the duty to deliver and for breach of contract (see below).

The contract with Chloe appears to be difficult in several respects, not least of them being that she is receiving damaged goods at an amount of 40 from the 60 she has ordered. She has made a down payment for only 30 and Slimbo has inserted a 'reservation of title' clause reserving his rights of disposal over the goods until the goods are fully paid for. Moreover, Chloe has only paid for 30 on a down payment basis whereas she receives 40 (that rightfully belonged to Bill if they had been delivered in good order in accordance with his contract). So the problems Chloe faces are that there has been an 'under' delivery of her contracted amount, unknown to her at delivery the goods are damaged (we are not told how badly). There is a 'reservation of title clause' which may prevent her obtaining title to the goods as against Slimbo's receiver in bankruptcy and lastly, the goods by rights should have gone to Bill.

To Chloe there has been an 'actual' delivery whilst to Bill, it can be argued there has been a 'constructive delivery' in that the goods to complete his contract were delivered to a contractor. It may be that Bill will choose to allege negligence against Harry, the independent carrier; particularly as Harry has damaged goods in his care and in transit to Bill. It would appear that the relationship between Slimbo and Harry may be a contractual contract of agency and Harry appears to be obeying instructions from Slimbo - for example, he delivers the 40 widgets destined for Bill, to Chloe. It could be argued, that on the contrary, Harry is the agent of the buyers herein; and that once goods in a deliverable state are available at Slimbo's premises the latter has discharged the duty imposed upon him by s27 SOGA, ie 'It is the duty of the seller to deliver the goods and of the buyer to accept and pay for them.' This would appear to be inconclusive as delivery appears to be conditional upon being 'advised' and Slimbo has transferred the goods to Harry for onward transmission to Bill. 'Delivery' by the seller

QUESTION 5 (continued)

to the agent of the seller does not amount to delivery to a buyer because the seller is merely sending the goods to his alter ego. *Galbraith and Grant Ltd* v *Block* [1922] 2 KB 155.

Thus Bill's remedies lie against Slimbo for non-delivery and he will claim damages for this; such damages being a species of damages for breach of contract and the rules for claiming them are set out in SOGA s51 - the remedy applies whether or not property has passed to the buyer.

s51 (1)   Where the seller wrongfully neglects to deliver the goods ... the buyer may maintain an action against the seller for damages for non-delivery.

(2)   The measure of damages is the estimated loss directly and naturally resulting, in the ordinary course of events, from the seller's breach of contract.

However, as Slimbo is now insolvent this would appear to be a poor option; better that Bill sues the agent (Harry) and joins the seller in the action so that the agent will pay for damage to the goods from his insurance policy and seek an indemnity from the receivers of his principal.

Chloe's contract is the subject of a so-called Romalpa (i.e.: retention of title clause), emanating from *Aluminium Industrie* v *Romalpa Aluminium Ltd* [1976] 1 WLR 676 which is designed to reserve the property in the goods to the seller until the price is paid in full, notwithstanding the goods have been delivered to the buyer. Whilst in the practical sense the goods have been delivered to the premises belonging to Chloe's business, in the legal sense delivery (s27 SOGA) has not taken place. She has had no opportunity to inspect the goods and would not want damaged goods. She can therefore reject the goods and claim breach of contract under the same grounds as Bill, with the additional element that goods of insufficient quantity have been taken to her premises in breach of s30(1) SOGA 'where the seller delivers to the buyer a quantity of goods less than he contracted to sell, the buyer may reject them.' Moreover, as Slimbo has sold goods in the course of a business s14 SOGA implied conditions applies and Chloe can reject the goods as being 'not fit for their purpose' or of 'merchantable quality'. *Behrend & Co Ltd* v *Produce Brothers Co Ltd* [1920] 3 KB 530.

Chloe will obviously have to pursue her claim in priority with other creditors in Slimbo's insolvency, as there is no contractual link between her and Harry and the goods. She cannot pursue the options available to Bill.

QUESTION 6

General Comment

A straight forward question that deals with export trade and manufacturers' liabilities divided into three sections that the well prepared candidate should have relatively little difficulty with. The first part deals with the passing of risk and property under a C + F Contract, the second part deals with an ex-ship contract and the seller's rights to intercept the goods placed on ship under such a contract and thirdly, the final part of the question deals with the nature of a contract for re-sale made by a retailer and whether or not the original seller/manufacturer has any responsibility to the ultimate consumer.

Skeleton Answer

a) Definition of C + F, effects thereof, documents of title in relation thereto, frustration of contract by natural disaster.

b) Ex ship contracts - definitions thereof, implications of such contract, rights and duties of parties to C + F contract.

c) Defects in products. Consumer Protection Act - SOGA 1979 s14 (2) + (3).

Suggested Solution

a) In this contract we are told that the wheat has been shipped from New York on 1st June and that four days later the ship sinks; two days subsequent to the sinking the seller (Selim) tenders the shipping documents to the buyer (Barbara). The contract has been made 'C and F'. This stands for 'cort and freight'; the basis of the agreement is that the seller has to arrange the carriage of the goods to the named foreign port of destination at his (ie the seller's) expense but not at his risk (which latter ceases when he places the goods on board ship at the place of shipment). In one aspect the 'C + F' contract differs from the Cif contract (namely the seller does not have to arrange marine insurance, but if he does then this must be paid for at his expense) in all other respects it is the same.

The essential element that is missing then in the contract between 'B' and 'S' is that of insurance, normally the proper division of responsibilities is resolved by Cif contracts (here the (i) stands for insurance). Sometimes a 'C and F' contract will contain words such as 'insurance to be effected by the buyer' and it has been held that these words are not merely declaratory but amount to a contractual obligation on the part of the buyer to take out the usual insurance policy (see *Reinhart Co* v *Joshua Hoyle & Sons Ltd* [1961] 1 Lloyd's Rep 346). So we are presented with a situation where the goods are placed on the ship and ostensibly where the seller has discharged his responsibilities. In the absence of express agreement to the matter of insurance it must be decided who bears the loss of the wheat and also whether or not the seller is lawfully entitled to tender documents of title after the loss of the goods in ocean transit and thus claim the purchase price of the goods.

It has been held that even though goods are lost in a Cif contract the seller still has the lawful right to tender the documents of title and to claim the purchase price - even in one case where the seller 'knew' the goods were lost when he offered the documents (*Manbre Saccharine* v *Corn Products Co*). As already stated, the same principles apply in Cif and C and F contracts and thus the tender of documents to claim the price is lawful. The buyer's usual remedy is a claim against the carrier either on the basis of the latter's negligence or because the buyer is an assignee of the bill of lading. There is one (albeit small) possibility of a claim by 'B' against 'S' here and that is that if, contrary to the terms of section 32(3) of Sale of Goods Act 1979 the seller has failed to give adequate notice of the shipment of the goods to enable the buyer sufficient time to insure the goods, then the goods would travel, exceptionally at the seller's and not the buyer's risk - but this does not appear to be the case as Barbara's claim will be against the carriers.

b) This contract is expressed to be 'ex-ship' Mangel and is for 1,000 gallons of perfume. There appears to be some dispute about a previous contract for shipment by Selim to Betty of cork mats, and in respect of these Selim appears to be an 'unpaid seller'; Betty's excuse for not paying being related directly to her inability to resell goods delivered to her under a contract of sale.

QUESTION 6 (continued)

The Judicial Committee of the Privy Council examined and defined the meaning of an 'ex-ship' contract as denoting 'that the seller has to cause delivery to be made to the buyer from a ship which has arrived at the port of delivery and has reached a place in which is usual for the delivery of goods of the kind in question.'

The clause is also contained and defined in the Incoterms that regulate such international shipping contracts. The nature of the obligations under the term 'ex ship' are that the seller has to pay the freight and the buyer is only bound to pay the purchase price if actual delivery of the goods is made at the stipulated port of delivery' thus if for example, the goods are lost in transit the buyer is not obliged to pay the price upon tender of the documents and can in certain cases claim the price he paid in advance.

Thus the property in the goods will only pass (unless otherwise agreed) when the goods are handed over to the buyer after arrival of the ship at the agreed port of destination.

The seller herein appears to have exercised his right of 'stoppage in transit in accordance with section 45 Sale of Goods Act 1979'; under this section three conditions must be present before the right to stop in transit arises. Namely

1)   The goods must be in transit and the goods are in transit when they have passed out of possession of the seller into possession of an independent carrier.

2)   The seller must be an unpaid seller.

3)   The buyer must be insolvent.

All three of these conditions appear to have been satisfied in particular the third one as under s61(4) SOGA 1979 a person is 'deemed to be insolvent with the meaning of the Act if he has either ceased to pay his debts in the ordinary course of business or he cannot pay his debts as they become due ...'. The goods are in transit according to section 45(1) 'goods are deemed to be in transit from the time when they are delivered to a carrier ... for the purpose of transmission to the buyer ... until the buyer or his agent in that behalf, takes delivery of them from the carrier.

As delivery has not taken place this appears to be the valid exercise of the remedy of stoppage in transit by Selim which Betty will have no defence against.

c)   Selim has contracted to sell 60 chainsaws to Billy who in turn has re-sold them to Tom; it appears that the goods have not been delivered to Billy who has instructed Selim to act on his behalf and deliver them on to Tom. When, six weeks later Tom's customers are injured by defects in the saws, Tom takes the prudent step of re-calling them and he also reimburses his customers and returns the goods to Billy from whom he bought them. We are concerned therefore with the duties of the seller and the retailer and possibly also the manufacturer (we do not know if Selim has manufactured the goods).

There are statutory duties imposed upon sellers under s14(2) and (3) Sale of Goods 1979 which are 'inalienable'; the seller is liable in this respect for 'merchantable quality' and 'fitness for purpose' without proof of lack of care on his part, in other words liability is strict. A common law expedient available to a seller who receives defective goods from a manufacturer and sells them on to the buyer is that of breach of implied warranty. If the buyer sues the seller fro breach of warranty of fitness for purpose then the seller may sue his manufacturer and in turn claim an indemnity (eg *Dodd* v *Wilson* [1946] 2 All ER 691).

Product liability is now covered by The Consumer Protection Act 1987 and the basic principles of protection for consumers are contained therein. These are that any person who suffers damage which is caused by a defective product, is entitled to sue the producer without being required to prove fault. S 5(1) of the CPA defines damage as 'death or personal injury or any loss of damage to any property (including land)'.

QUESTION 6 (continued)

It appears therefore, that Tom can return the goods to Bill and claim damages under SOGA 1979 ss14(2)(3). Additionally, the two injured customers can claim against the manufacturer under CPA 1987 if they can prove their injuries resulted from the defects in the product. Billy will be entitled to recover the price paid for the products from the manufacturer and damages for loss of profit.

QUESTION 7

General Comment

A question that deals with hire-purchase agreements and the implied terms and conditions therein; analogous to those relating to title, merchantable quality, etc contained in the Sale of Goods Act 1979. Questions of ownership and title need to be resolved as does the lien purportedly being exercised by Xerxes until monies for repair are paid. Also some element of exclusion clauses is contained, and the validity, reasonableness and legality of the clause needs to be referred to in the light of the UCTA and the attempt to exclude the statutory simplified conditions.

Skeleton Answer

1.   HP generally - ownership, title and the implied conditions in the HP contract.

2.   DCS regulated agreements, the credit-broker as agent of the creditor, rights and duties of creditors and debtors inter se.

3.   Passing of title under HP agreements that have not been completed, private sales.

4.   Exclusion clauses UCTA, documents of title.

5.   Remedies, liens, misrepresentation.

Suggested Solution

We are asked to advise Hiram (H). Delbert (D) is a used car dealer, presumably he has some knowledge and expertise that he applies when purchasing secondhand vehicles for re-sale to his clients. Additionally, in his trade he will have some knowledge of the proof of ownership and documents of title that are necessary to trade in secondhand vehicles. It is reasonable to assume that, with experience of this kind of motor vehicle sales, he will make (or should have made) some enquiries as to whether or not the vehicle was changed or encumbered in any way when he purchased the 1966 Ford Consul he is advertising, from Robert (R).

D has advertised the 1966 Ford Consul as being 'in perfect condition as the day she was made'; it seems unlikely that he will believe in the truth of this claim if (as is usual) he has inspected a vehicle which is 24 years old and has recently been in what we are told was a 'serious accident'. It seems unlikely (though possible) that the vehicle has had only 'one owner' as claimed by D to induce Hiram (H) to purchase the vehicle; the vehicle is 24 years old, but we know that R had it on hire-purchase from the same finance company that D acts as credit broker for, namely Finco Ltd. No finance company will agree to Hire Purchase over 24 years; so R could logically not have been the only owner. In other words D it appears, made two serious misrepresentations about the condition of the vehicle in written form when he advertises, knowing or suspecting his statement in this respect to be grossly misleading at least; and secondly, when he makes oral representations that the Ford has had only one owner.

Additionally, if he has made the usual enquiries and examined the log-book and title documents, he will not only know that his statements are untrue; but will probably have some inkling or direct knowledge that the vehicle was under HP from Finco to R.

We are confronted here by two separate hire purchase agreements in relation to the same vehicle; two agreements made at different times and to different 'owners' of the Ford, but both with the same creditor, Finco Ltd. In the present case D appears to have acted as a 'credit broker' by introducing H to Finco and arranging HP terms for H's purchase from D of the car. In this respect the arrangement would be a debtor-creditor-supplier agreement with A, Finco and D fulfilling respective roles. Moreover, the agreement will almost certainly be a 'regulated' agreement under the terms of the CCA 1974 s13 (for the present purposes we can assume that D and Finco are 'connected' and have a 'pre-existing arrangement' as to the hire purchase D arranges). We are not told the amount of the hire purchase or the repayment periods or amounts, but we can assume that the upper limit of the total hire purchase does not exceed £15,000 and that s8 (regulated agreements) CCA 1974 applies.

Some general points about the nature of both hire purchase agreements can be made at this point to enable us to fully explore the questions of ownership title and lien that arise subsequent to D selling the Ford to R.

QUESTION 7 (continued)

The essential nature of a hire purchase contract as regulated by the CCA 1974 has been described as being a 'bailment' of the goods (ie a delivery of possession of goods plus the grant of an option to purchase the goods (Sir Gordon Barrie - Commercial Law 6th Edn)). The working of the modern hire purchase contract was described in graphic terms by Lord Denning in *Bridge v Campbell Discount Co Ltd* [1962] AC 600

> 'It is in effect, though not in law, a mortgage of goods ... the finance house has become the owner of goods who lets them out on hire. So it buys the goods from the dealer and lets them out on hire to the appellant (bailee).'

A hire purchase contract is not a sale of goods because under hire purchase the customer is never bound to buy and only becomes the owner when all the instalments are paid and he has exercised the option to purchase (generally speaking).

Hire purchase contracts confer advantages on both parties: the bailee gets possession of the goods and the period of hire to pay for them with the option to own them at the end of the period, the bailer 'sells' the goods and receives interest on the hire purchase price. However, HP contracts also incur liabilities (and duties) and penalties for the breach of these.

The main duties of the bailee include to pay the instalments, to take reasonable care of the goods and not to relinquish possession to any third party, the principal obligations of the creditor include the implied terms as to fitness, title, quality etc (Supply of Goods (Implied Terms) Act 1973).

Before advising H, it is necessary to look at the chain of events that resulted in his taking the car on hire purchase from Finco after being introduced to them by D who is in effect a credit broker for Finco. The original HP agreement between R and Finco meant that Finco is the original creditor and R the original debtor. R damages and repairs the car and sells it (presumably for cash) to D. D acquires the documents of title, but Finco would not appear therein. R is in breach of his duty to Finco not to relinquish possession of the hire vehicle; he has at that stage no rights of ownership and no rights of disposal. We are not told if R has continued to pay instalments after selling to D or if he has discharged his debt to Finco. We can assume he has done neither of these. In any event R appears to be in breach of his duty to take reasonable care of the goods and has damaged them in an accident and resorted to re-pairing them himself. The debtor is not liable for fair wear and tear but the onus is on him during the currency of the agreement if the goods are damaged, to show that he has taken reasonable care of them; *Joseph Travers & Sons v Cooper* [1915] 1 KB 73 88.

Hiram takes the car following the misrepresentations by D about its condition, ownership and his (D's) title to sell to H. D also introduces H to Finco and Finco enter a second HP agreement with H (the first being with R) for the hire of the Ford. Finco already own the vehicle and are creditors to R. H signs an HP agreement which includes an exclusion clause.

As a purchaser from R, D could possibly have got good title to the vehicle if he knew nothing of the HP agreement between R and Finco. However, the fact that D is a secondhand car dealer denies him the 'special protection' afforded to a 'private purchaser' (someone who does not carry on a business as a dealer in motor vehicles or of providing finance for hire purchase transactions in motor vehicles) under Part III Hire Purchase Act 1964. Section 27 HPA 1964 Pt III provides where the bailee of a motor vehicle 'disposes' of it to a private purchaser who takes it in good faith and without notice of the hire purchase agreement 'such disposition' has effect as if the creditor's title to the vehicle had been vested in the debtor' immediately before that disposition.

There is a wealth of case law on the subject of goods sold on hire purchase being 'disposed' of during the currency of the agreement by the bailee; it would appear that by his breaches R has terminated his agreement with Finco and the latter are entitled to recover possession of the vehicle and to sue R for damages to their property through his negligence; *Ballett v Mingay* [1943] KB 281. D appears to be the agent of Finco as he seems to have a 'pre-arranged' finance agreement to recommend customers to them (i.e. D is a credit broker under the CCA 1974).

D's misrepresentations are subject to the Misrepresentation Act 1967 s3 (which governs exclusion clauses excluding liability for misrepresentation), in that they induce H to purchase the car and appear to substantially influence his decision. As D's principal, Finco appears to be liable for these misrepresentations; when H sought HP from them they would have checked their records and seen that they already owned the Ford and that an HP agreement already existed in R's favour. D has 'special' skill and knowledge upon which H appears to

QUESTION 7 (continued)

rely - albeit that caveat emptor and the SOGA implied conditions as to merchantable quality apply - these are displaced by D's skill and knowledge, his misrepresentations and the fact that the defects do not appear to have been evident on a 'reasonable' inspection by H prior to purchase.

The exclusion clause inserted by Finco appears to be invalid, as they know or should reasonably know, that R has an HP agreement on the Ford which they own already and in any event it does not appear to satisfy the 'reasonableness' tests set out in the UCTA 1977 (ss6 & 11). Additionally, they may be denied protection under HPA 1964 Part III because they provide finance for the purchase of vehicles and may be a 'dealer' thereunder.

Hiram appears to be within his rights to terminate the agreement by giving notice to the credit broker (D) as he has done; in *Financings Ltd* v *Stimson* [1962] 3 All ER 386 Lord Denning expressed the view that the dealer was agent of the finance company for the purposes of receiving notice of the customer's revocation of his offer; so that communication by the customer to the dealer of his desire to withdraw his offer is equivalent to communication to the finance company; ss57, 69 and 102 CCA 1974. Under the principle that the principal is liable for any statements made by the agent during any 'antecedent negotiations' (including any representations made by the negotiator to the debtor (s56(4) CCA)), Finco will be liable to H for D's misrepresentations.

The lien purportedly exercised by Xerxes over the car for repairs may well be valid as, during the currency of an HP agreement, the hirer has the implied authority to deliver the goods to a third party for repair provided the act is reasonably incidental to his use of the goods. So in *Green* v *All Motors Ltd* [1917] KB 625 it was decided that a lien to secure repairing charges was effective against the owner.

Thus, H should confirm the cancellation of the agreement in writing to Finco at their offices, he can then pursue the question of damages for breach of implied conditions as to title (s12) and merchantable quality and fitness for purpose (s14) Supply of Goods (Implied Terms) Act 1973 against Finco as they have allowed D to act as their agent and are liable for his and their own misrepresentations. The exclusion clause will almost certainly be regarded as 'unreasonable' (UCTA) and unenforceable. Xerxes will be able to exercise his lien over the goods for repairs.

QUESTION 8

General Comment

A two part question that deals with hire purchase agreements in both parts, the first part deals with the formalities necessary for the formation of such an agreement and the consumer's rights of cancellation in relation to new goods sold by a hirer, and the second part deals with the rights of ownership of secondhand goods sold under hire purchase.

A relatively straightforward question providing the candidate pays attention to detail and observes the subtle but important differences between the two parts of the question. It is also important to observe the D-C-S nature of the agreements.

Skeleton Answer

a) 1   Hire purchase generally - new goods - implied terms.

    2   Debtor-Creditor-Supplier/Debtor-Creditor agreements.

    3   Requirements/formalities for HP agreements.

    4   Cancellation.

    5   Relationship between Debtor/Creditor and Debtor/Supplier.

b) 1   HP generally - secondhand goods.

    2   Formalities.

    3   Part payment. Possession and ownership differentiated.

    4   Protected goods.

    5   Re-possession - entry into premises - termination.

Suggested Solution

In this question we are asked to advise Horatio (H) who has entered into two separate agreements with the Finance-U Co to acquire goods which are supplied by Denden Plc. Both agreements appear to be hire purchase agreements and therefore their formation and the obligations of the respective parties under them are regulated by Part V of the Consumer Credit Act 1974.

a)   Under the first agreement H has entered into a hire purchase agreement to purchase a new refrigerator at a price of £300, the goods to be supplied by Denden Plc and the finance under the hire purchase to be provided by Finance-U Co. Certain agreements are exempt from the provisions of the CCA 1974 - most notably the 50 called 'small' agreements for restricted use credit (i.e. those regulated hire purchase agreements which do not require the hirer to make payments exceeding £50 s17(1)). We are given no information about the payments to be made by H; but it would appear that this agreement exceeds the £50 upper limit and the agreement is therefore not exempt under s17(1).

        It is important at this stage to classify the agreements that H has entered into in order that one can fully advise him in respect of his rights and responsibilities thereunder. The 'agreement' in respect of the refrigerator appears to fall within the classification of a Debtor-Creditor-Supplier agreement. In essence this means that either the creditor is also the supplier of the goods or services or has an existing or contemplated business connection with the supplier. The other kind of agreement (that has not been entered into by H) recognised by the CCA ss12 and 13 is a debtor-creditor agreement where the creditor merely supplies the debtor with the needed credit facilities but the creditor is not also the supplier and has no business connection or contemplated business connection with the supplier.

        As already stated, this arrangement appears to be a hire purchase agreement; such an agreement is defined by s189 CCA 1974, as being:

QUESTION 8 (continued)

'an agreement, other than a conditional sale agreement under which goods are bailed in return for periodical payments by the bailee and the property in the goods will pass to the bailee if the terms of the agreement are complied with and the bailee exercises an option to purchase the goods'.

Often the retailer may choose to provide the finance for the agreement, but in the alternative a tripartite arrangement may be formed when the retailer sells the goods to a finance house and the finance house lets the goods out to the consumer on hire purchase terms. This has the net result that the finance house has in effect, made a secured loan to the debtor.

The questions here are whether or not the hire purchase agreement has been made in accordance with the appropriate regulations and formalities and secondly, whether H has any rights of cancellation when (two days after visiting the shop) he decides he does not want the fridge after all.

From the facts given, the agreement appears to be a 'regulated' agreement under s189 of the CCA 1974 and therefore must comply with the requirements of the Act in relation to disclosure of information, form and content, signature, copies and notices of cancellation rights. Section 60 of the CCA required detailed regulations to be made about the specified information to be included in the prescribed manner in documents for the making of 'regulated' agreements. The regulations made under s60 are known as the Consumer Credit (Agreements) Regulations 1983 and they provide that the agreement must be clearly legible and state the following information.

a)   The amount of the credit or credit limit

b)   The total charge for credit

c)   Amounts and timings of repayment

d)   The Annual Percentage Rate (APR)

e)   Details of any security provided by the debtor

Additionally, the implied terms and conditions contained in the SOGA 1979 ss12-15 are substantially repeated in relation to hire purchase contracts in the Supply of Goods (Implied Terms) Act 1973 (as amended) so that the hirer is in essentially the same position as regards title description, quality, fitness and sales by samples.

In most respects the apparent 'hire purchase' agreement entered into by H does not comply with the statutory requirements; in sequence these are as follows: Section 61(1)a CCA requires the agreement to be signed by the debtor or hirer personally and it must also be signed by or on behalf of the owner or creditor. Improper signatures means the agreement is improperly executed. Indeed the Consumer Credit (Agreements) Regulations 1983 prescribe a standard format for such signature boxes and additionally, if the agreement is cancellable, they cover a 'notice to cancel' box.

Sections 62 and 63 of the CCA contain detailed provisions in relation to copies of agreements to be provided to consumers. The debtor should receive at least one (and usually two copies) of the agreement and any other documents referred to in it; no details are given about whether or not the 'agreement' is cancellable, so one must assume it is bearing in mind H's actions. Breach of any requirements as to copies renders the agreement improperly executed (ss61-63). This agreement appears to be unexecuted at the time H was in the shop, we are not told if he signed it but can assume he did not. The agreement consists only of 'the basic terms', presumably repayments, price, APR etc and a note stating that the agreement is on Finance-U Co's usual terms.

H is given no notice of his cancellation rights under the special provisions thereon contained in s61(1)(a) to ensure the debtor is informed about his right to cancel. If the agreement is cancellable all the relevant copies under ss62 and 63 must be sent/given and contain a notice in the prescribed form setting out the rights of cancellation. A cancellable agreement is improperly executed if the

QUESTION 8 (continued)

requirements as to cancellation notices are not met; these requirements under the Consumer Credit (Cancellation Notices and Copies of Documents) Regulations 1983 require a notice of cancellation rights to indicate:

i)   The right of the debtor to cancel

ii)   How and when to cancel it

iii)   The name and address of a person to whom notice of cancellation may be given.

In conclusion then, this appears to be an attempt to make a regulated hire purchase agreement which fails for several reasons. Most notably, neither the debtor or creditor appear to have signed the agreement or the copies, secondly, the requirements of copies for what appears to be an unexecuted agreement (2nd copy within 7 days of the agreement being executed). Assuming the agreement to be cancellable no notice in the prescribed form about cancellation rights is contained in the agreement or sent to H. Lastly, the agreement is signed ex post facto to H's purported cancellation over the telephone by Finance-U Co (the creditor).

The agreement is in breach of the CCA in all these respects and therefore is improperly executed; the effect of an improperly executed agreement is that it can only be enforceable by an order of the court s65(1) CCA 1974. The court will look at culpability and the loss to the parties; in this case it appears to be Denden and Finance-U Co who are at fault and who fail to comply with the formalities. Accordingly, H will have effectively cancelled the agreement and it will not be enforced by the courts against him. Notice of cancellation is served by the telephone call under s69 CCA where the debtor or hirer can serve notice 'however expressed' on the agent of the debtor or hirer - no special or mandatory form of notice is required. There is no question of repayment of monies or liens as the fridge has not been delivered and no monies have been paid.

b)   In this case, we are again presented with a CCA regulated hire purchase agreement in respect of a secondhand lawn mower. However, the circumstances of the making of the agreement are very different and the questions of ownership, title and re-possession need to be settled.

In simple legal terms a hire purchase agreement is a bailment of goods (ie a delivery of possession of goods) plus the grant of an option to purchase. To be afforded the protection of the CCA such agreements should comply with the formalities that they be in writing, signed by both parties, contain all the agreed terms and that the correct copies and notices of provisions are completed. There appears to be some attempt here to infer that the agreement may be a 'cancellable' agreement because we are given few details about its exact nature but we are told that the agreement (top and carbon copies) are sent by Finance-U Co to H's home for him to peruse, and two days later he signs them at Denden's premises.

Whilst it is possible with some certainty to regard Denden Plc as the agent (and negotiator) for the creditor (ie Finance-U Co) it is almost impossible, bearing in mind the limited information about the formation of the agreement provided, to determine whether the agreement is cancellable under the four requirements necessary under s67 CCA 1974. We are not told whether any oral representations are made by the supplier or creditor, so under the fourth provision of s67 CCA it would appear that the agreement is prima facie not a cancellable one and the fact that H signs at Denden's premises is in this respect immaterial. He has had time to peruse the agreements and raise any queries and does not appear to be pressurised at the time of signing by his unfamiliar surroundings or sales techniques.

The problem then concerns the respective rights, duties and responsibilities of the parties (debtor-creditor and supplier) following the making of a valid agreement.

Horatio has paid £200 of the total hire purchase price of £480, this means the goods have not yet passed into his ownership (they will not do so until all instalments have been paid and the option to purchase exercised). However, the goods are protected goods under s90(1) CCA 1974. Section 90 states that goods are 'protected goods' at any time when:

QUESTION 8 (continued)

a)   The debtor is in breach of a regulated hire purchase or conditional sales agreement relating to goods; and

b)   The debtor has paid to the creditor one-third or more of the total price of the goods; and

c)   The property of the goods remains in the creditor.

Section 90(1)

This section is designed to protect the debtor against unscrupulous 'snatch-back' by the creditor and the debtor is afforded three-fold protection by the CCA so that before 'snatch-back' can occur notice must be given, any entry onto debtor's premises is restricted and the goods in any event may be 'protected'.

Under a hire purchase agreement the parties have certain rights, duties and obligations. The implied condition on the part of the creditor/credit broker is that the hirer will 'enjoy quiet possession of the goods's8 Supply of Goods (Implied Terms) Act 1973. However, there is a corresponding implied obligation on the bailee of goods to use reasonable care in looking after the goods, the debtor will be liable in damages if he chooses not to exercise his option to purchase or the contract is determined for non-payment etc. If the goods are damaged during the currency of the agreement the onus is on the debtor to show he has taken reasonable care of them (*Joseph Travers & Sons* v *Cooper* [1915] 1 KB 73 88). The debtor may be liable in damages for the loss caused to the creditor.

As already mentioned the lawn mower is 'protected' under s90 CCA as more than half the hire purchase price has been paid. Contravention of s90 means that the agreement is terminated, the debtor is released from all liability, the debtor is entitled to recover from the creditor all sums paid by the debtor under the agreement (s91 CCA 1974). Section 90 does not apply where the debtor has himself terminated the agreement or if the debtor agrees to the re-possession at the time.

It can be argued that by non-payment of two instalments H is in breach of the agreement and has thus terminated it, entitling Finance-V Co's representative to re-possess. However, his illness may have led to this as an oversight and additionally, he has not overtly repudiated the agreement, by for example, writing to the creditor or credit broker. In *Financings Ltd* v *Baldock* the Court of Appeal stated that mere failure to pay two instalments does not amount to repudiation to entitle the creditor to re-possess. The creditor in this case could only claim the arrears and damages for non-payment of the arrears.

The creditor or owner is not entitled to terminate the contract or re-possess the goods unless written notice has been shown of the termination (usually at least seven days default notice) ss87 and 92(1) CCA. 'The creditor is not entitled to enter any premises' to take possession of goods the subject of a regulated hire purchase agreement 'without a court order' and the debtor cannot recover possession of protected goods without a court order s90(2).

The hurricane that damages the lawn mower is described as a freak. A barn may not be the safest place to keep the (lawn mower - but the agreement has not been terminated by default (only two instalments not paid) or by notice. The goods are protected and Finance-U Co's representative gets no consent from H for re-possession at the time of his illegal entry onto H's premises. Thus the re-possession is illegal and H can treat the agreement as terminated and reclaim all £200 paid thereunder. He must make the goods available for collection but has no duty to delivery them himself to the creditor.

ORDER FORM

ELB PUBLICATIONS

ELB PUBLICATIONS	TEXTBOOKS Cost £	CASEBOOKS £	REVISION WORKBOOKS £	SUG. SOL. 1985/89 Cost £	SUG. SOL. 1990 Cost £
Administrative Law	17.95	18.95		14.95	3.00
Commercial Law Vol I	17.95	18.95		14.95	3.00
Vol II	16.95	18.95	9.95	14.95	3.00
Company Law	18.95	18.95	9.95	14.95	3.00
Conflict of Laws	17.95	16.95			
Constitutional Law	13.95	16.95	9.95	14.95	3.00
Contract Law	13.95	16.95	9.95	14.95	3.00
Conveyancing	16.95	16.95			
Criminal Law	13.95	16.95	9.95	14.95	3.00
Criminology	16.95				
European Community Law	17.95	16.95			3.00
English Legal System	13.95	14.95		*7.95	3.00
Equity and Trusts	13.95	18.95	9.95	14.95	3.00
Evidence	17.95	17.95	9.95	14.95	3.00
Family Law	16.95	18.95	9.95	14.95	3.00
Jurisprudence	14.95		9.95	14.95	3.00
Labour Law	15.95				
Land Law	13.95	18.95	9.95	14.95	3.00
Public International Law	18.95	16.95	9.95	14.95	3.00
Revenue Law	16.95	18.95	9.95	14.95	3.00
Roman Law	19.95				
Succession	16.95	17.95	9.95	14.95	3.00
Tort	13.95	18.95	9.95	14.95	3.00

CPE PUBLICATIONS

CPE PUBLICATIONS	Cost £
Criminal Law	13.95
Constitutional & Administrative Law	13.95
Contract Law	13.95
Equity and Trusts	13.95
Land Law	13.95
Tort	13.95

BAR PUBLICATIONS

BAR PUBLICATIONS	Cost £	SUG. SOL. 1985/89 Cost £	SUG. SOL. 1990 Cost £
Conflict of Laws	16.95	† 3.95	3.95
European Community Law & Human Rights	17.95	† 3.95	3.95
Evidence	17.95	14.95	3.95
Family Law	16.95	14.95	3.95
General Paper I	19.95	14.95	3.95
General Paper II	19.95	14.95	3.95
Law of International Trade			
Practical Conveyancing	16.95	14.95	3.95
Procedure	19.95	14.95	3.95
Revenue Law	16.95	14.95	3.95
Sale of Goods and Credit	17.95	14.95	3.95

*1987-1989 papers only † 1988 and 1989 papers only

SOLICITORS' FINAL

SOLICITORS' FINAL	TEXTBOOKS Cost £	REVISION WORKBOOKS Cost £	PACKS (a) Winter Cost £	PACKS (a) Summer Cost £	SINGLE PAPERS (b) Winter Cost £	SINGLE PAPERS (b) Summer Cost £
Accounts	14.95	9.95	14.95	14.95	2.25	2.25
Business Organisations & Insolvency	14.95		11.95	§ 11.95	2.25	2.25
Consumer Protection & Employment Law	14.95		11.95	§ 11.95	2.25	2.25
Conveyancing I & II	14.95		14.95	14.95	2.25	2.25
Family Law	14.95		14.95	14.95	2.25	2.25
Litigation	14.95		14.95	14.95	2.25	2.25
Wills, Probate & Administration	14.95	9.95	14.95	14.95	2.25	2.25
Final Exam Papers (Set) (All Papers) 1989				9.95		
Final Exam Papers (Set) (All Papers) 1990			9.95	9.95		

INSTITUTE OF LEGAL EXECUTIVES

INSTITUTE OF LEGAL EXECUTIVES	Cost £
Company & Partnership Law	18.95
Constitutional Law	13.95
Contract Law	13.95
Criminal Law	13.95
Equity and Trusts	13.95
European Law & Practice	17.95
Evidence	17.95
Land Law	13.95
Revenue Law	16.95
Tort	13.95

§ Limited to new syllabus from Summer 1986.

(a) Packs consist of either collected Winter or Summer papers. They change in April to include the previous Summer & Winter papers respectively.

(b) Single papers are published in April & October and are the previous Winter & Summer papers respectively, together with final examination papers.

HLT PUBLICATIONS

All HLT Publications have two important qualities. First, they are written by specialists, all of whom have direct practical experience of teaching the syllabus. Second, all Textbooks are reviewed and updated each year to reflect new developments and changing trends.

They are used widely by students at polytechnics and colleges throughout the United Kingdom and overseas.

A comprehensive range of titles is covered by the following classifications.

- **TEXTBOOKS**

- **CASEBOOKS**

- **SUGGESTED SOLUTIONS**

- **REVISION WORKBOOKS**

The books listed overleaf can be ordered through your local bookshops or obtained direct from the publisher using this order form. Telephone, Fax, or Telex orders will also be accepted. Quote your Access or Visa card numbers for priority orders. To order direct from publisher please enter cost of titles you require, fill in despatch details and send it with your remittance to The HLT Group Ltd.

| **Please complete Order Form overleaf** |

DETAILS FOR DESPATCH OF PUBLICATIONS
Please insert your full name below

Please insert below the style in which you would like the correspondence from the Publisher addressed to you
TITLE Mr, Miss etc.   INITIALS   SURNAME/FAMILY NAME

Address to which study material is to be sent (please ensure someone will be present to accept delivery of your Publications).

If you wish to order by post this may be done direct from the Publisher. Postal charges are as follows:

POSTAGE & PACKING
You are welcome to purchase study material from the Publisher at 200 Greyhound Road, London W14 9RY, during normal working hours.

UK   - Orders over £30: no charge. Orders below £30: £2.00. Single paper (last exam only): 40p
OVERSEAS   - See table below

The Publisher cannot accept responsibility in respect of postal delays or losses in the postal systems.
DESPATCH All cheques must be cleared before material is despatched.

SUMMARY OF ORDER

Date of order:

Add postage and packing:

Cost of publications ordered:
UNITED KINGDOM:

	TEXTS		Suggested Solutions (last Exam only)
OVERSEAS:	One	Each Extra	
European Community	£3.00	£0.50	£1.00
Eire	£7.50	£0.50	£1.00
East Europe & North America	£8.50	£1.00	£1.50
South East Asia	£10.00	£1.50	£1.50
Australia / New Zealand	£12.00	£3.50	£1.50
Other Countries (Africa, India etc)	£11.00	£3.00	£1.50

Total cost of order: £

Please ensure that you enclose a cheque or draft payable to The HLT Group Ltd for the above amount, or charge to ☐ ◣ ☐ VISA

Card Number ☐☐☐☐☐☐☐☐☐☐☐☐☐☐

Expiry Date _____   Signature _____